IDEA TO PROJECT

Idea to Project
A guide to organise your thoughts easily

INES LOPEZ

Idea to Project by Ines Lopez is licensed under a Creative Commons Attribution-ShareAlike 4.0 International License

All the commercial brands mentioned in this book are property of their respective owners.

ISBN: 9798364790453

TABLE OF CONTENTS

1	Introduction	1
2	Defining your idea	5
	2.1 Define the benefits map for your project	8
	2.2 Software you can use	9
	2.3 How to use this map	10
3	Identify what your project entails	12
	3.1 Software you can use	16
4	The mother of all project documents	17
	4.1 Sequencing your tasks	17
	4.2 Tasks and time space	19
	4.3 Your project timeline	20
	4.4 Money time	24
	4.5 Software you can use	27
5	What comes next	29
6	Your mindset	32
	6.1 Your mind is not your enemy	38
	6.2 The process delivers results in the long run	40
	6.3 Inner work is about taking responsibility	41
	6.4 There is always a lesson, a gift	43

6.5 Triggers are growth opportunities	44
6.6 You are working with invisible things	47
6.7 Finding kindness	48
About the author	51

1 INTRODUCTION

Welcome! You have an idea that inspires you and you just want to know how to make it a reality? You are in the right place. And thank you for giving me a chance to share with you the combination of my learnings over the last 10 years.

I believe project definition is the most exciting and interesting part of a project. I have worked on putting together the key knowledge and tools you will need to transform your idea into a workable project. Something that will be clear and structured, easy to follow for you and anyone else working with you on your idea.

This document is structured into the three deliverables that I believe are your best bang for your buck to define your project. Go through the chapters, watch the videos, do the exercises and by the end of it you will have:

- A simple benefits map to represent the good stuff your project is going to create. This is very useful to keep you motivated and also build support for your new adventure.

- A diagram that enables you to see all the type of tasks your project will require. With this tool you will understand whether you are going to need to outsource or ask for support. It can also help you assess if your idea is too complex and you should break it into several projects instead of trying to do it all at once.

- A timeline (sometimes referred as Gantt chart) showing your tasks organised in time and in sequence. This will be your go to tool to keep track of the project.

To produce those items I have used a mixed of different online systems, all free at the moment of writing:

- Miro (www.miro.com), a platform to create visual graphics in an easy way.

- ClickUp (www.clickup.com), a great system to organise and keep track of your tasks and projects.

I have created videos on how I have used them. You can access that material through the QR code or in the website

https://ineslopez.gumroad.com/l/additional.

Please note I don't have any affiliation with these brands. I used them because they get the job I want done but it is totally up to you whether you want to use them or not. You can do all the exercises I propose with just pen and paper if you prefer. The important thing is going through these chapters and organise your idea into a project no matter whether you record your results on paper or digitally.

I will keep the content simple because I strongly believe project management can and should be adapted to the project's circumstances. You don't need loads of documentation and complicated terminology to bring an idea to life. Just the basics to get you organised in a sensible way. And to do that you don't need to become a certified project manager.

If you are reading this and you feel your project is going to have a budget of millions and over 20 key stakeholders you may still benefit from this approach to get you going. However you may want to get some project management advice fairly soon. A project of that dimension should get into as much detail as

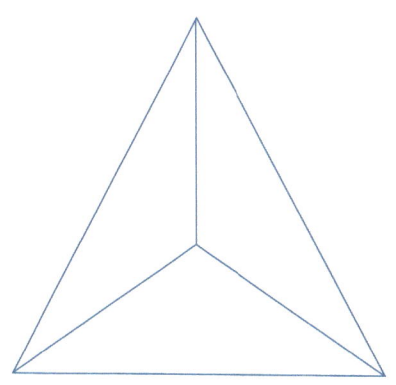

possible from the start so that it can run smoothly.

These pages have already helped people organise their thoughts into something easy to follow through, understand and communicate. My wish is that it can do the same for you too.

2 DEFINING YOUR IDEA

You probably have been having an idea floating in your brain for a while. One day you think about one aspect of it and a spark of inspiration on how to resolve it comes up. Then you wait, because life gets in the way, and a few days later the idea comes on, with another golden nugget attached to it. And you wonder, how can I make sense of all of this?

The first step is to define the goal of your idea.

Take a few deep breaths, connect with your idea and ask yourself: **What do I want to achieve?**

Write it down, trying to be concise. Think of the end result. To help you understand the purpose of each exercise I am going to use as an example the process I followed to create this "Idea to Project" content.

So in my case the goal I want to achieve is helping others to define projects so we can have more things happening in the world.

Now, **when do you want this result to happen?** Be specific by giving it a full date.

I want my project done by 20 November 2022. This refers to the deadline I have for myself to complete the tasks to get the project done. I consider my project complete when I have done all I need to get it available online.

Congrats! Now you know what you want to do and by when. If this sounds simple it is because to a high degree it is. One of the key aspects of a project is knowing what one is aiming for and giving it a timeframe. This helps you commit towards your idea so that every day you find the time to do what you need to make it happen.

The next aspect is to understand what your idea will bring in a few scenarios. This will help you get more clarity on the good stuff you are going to create by following up on your project. It can be a great tool to motivate you when things get busy. And you can use this information to be able to build support for your project.

To do this first answer the following questions:

1. What will your idea give to your business?

It will help me show my experience and knowledge in project management to position myself in the field. It will also create another income stream.

2. What will your idea give to you as a person/individual?

Sense of achievement by putting my skills and 10 years of experience to good use. I will feel more fulfilled helping people directly or indirectly with their projects.

3. What will your idea give to your clients, if you have them?

Knowledge and confidence to start their own projects. Being able to move forward with their ideas and dreams.

4. What will your idea give to your business team, if you have one?

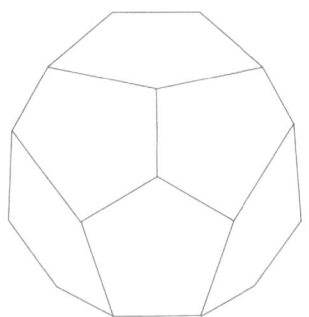

I don't have a team at the moment.

5. What will your idea give to the world?

More projects delivering good things are being brought to the world.

All the answers above are the key direct benefits

of your project. Your project will undoubtedly generate far more good stuff, you just have to identify it. And there is a very simple and engaging way of representing all this so the information is more easy to digest.

2.1 DEFINE DE BENEFITS MAP FOR YOUR PROJECT

What you are going to create is called a benefits map. You can find many types of templates, some more complex than others. I want to keep things simple so I have chosen a mind map structure style. It is easy to fill out, replicate and gets the job done. No need to overcomplicate things!

First you go back to the goal for your project, the first question you answered. Place it in the box on the left. That is the start of your benefits map. Then you ask yourself:

- What would this make/create/generate? and/or

- What impact would this have? What consequence will this have?

The answer (or answers if there is more than one) goes into different boxes that you place to the right of your initial box. It is like creating tree branches but in horizontal rather than vertical. You connect each box in the same branch with a line because these benefits relate to each other.

I wrote two questions to identify benefits because depending on the type of project one may be more applicable than the other, but the idea is always the same. From your answers you ask yourself the questions again and then take one of the results/ benefits you expect and write it in the following box, with a line connecting the two. You keep doing that until you don't have any more benefits.

Keep in mind you may have a benefit connecting to two different benefits, meaning you may have more than one line leaving and/or entering into a box. That is absolutely fine.

Below you can see an example of the type of benefits I aspire to generate with this "Idea to Project" adventure.

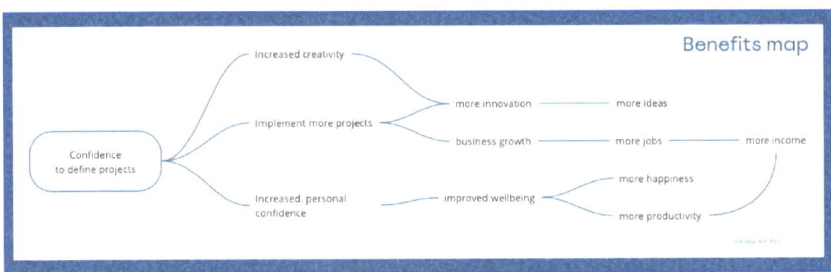

Now it's your turn.

2.2 SOFTWARE YOU CAN USE

You may want to make your benefits map in your laptop with some software. I can suggest the following free options (at the time of writing,

November 2022) that will help you put it together:

- Miro. With the free plan you can select the mind map template. This will allow you to create the graphic quite easily, like the one in the image above. In the additional material document you have the link to a video explaining how to do this.

- ClickUp. On their free version they have a mind map tool. This will allow you to put all the content for the benefits map and link them accordingly.

2.3 HOW TO USE THIS MAP

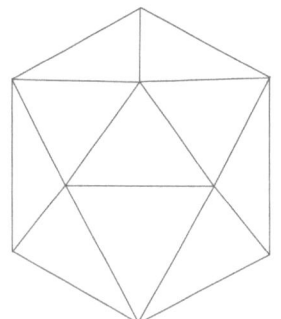

You can use it to motivate yourself on all the good your idea is going to create. This can help you push forward when things get a bit busy or complicated in your project.

Benefits maps are also excellent communications tools. They show all the positives of your project. Therefore you can use them to help people see why you love your project so much and why they should love it as well. It can help you gather support in many ways.

Pro tip
If you want to take this to the next level you can research online for benefits maps, business cases and monetisation of benefits.
In an ideal scenario you need to quantify the benefits of your project. This is one of the tools companies use to know whether a project is worth the money that it would cost to make it happen.

That to me is something fairly detailed and advanced. In short it is something like this. You will need to find relevant metrics for your benefits. The more the better, although it is understood that some benefits are qualitative (more about quality) and therefore can't be monetised because it is hard to measure them in detail.

In the example I provided you, one of the metrics I would need to identify is how much more productive someone is when their well being has improved. And what level of economic benefit (additional income that can be solely attributed to that change in wellbeing) has the company received as a result.
Then I would have to estimate how many people would be my customers (hence getting that benefit). Do some calculations with those values (and the rest of the economic values for all my benefits) to see what is the economic benefit of the project.
When I have completed the budget I will then compare the economic benefit with the predicted costs to see whether or not the project will generate more than it would take.

It is worth noting that sometimes projects get done regardless of their economic benefits. There are changes in laws and markets that may trigger projects for compliance or market survival. And there are also projects that happen because of a qualitative motivation, rather than quantitative. For example company benefits programs that may require a company to invest money in but they know employees will be happier, be more productive and stay longer in the company. I also believe with the recent changes in the way we work, more and more qualitative oriented projects are happening. This is great because money shouldn't be the only decision maker when doing a project!

3 IDENTIFY WHAT YOUR PROJECT ENTAILS

Congratulations! You have your goal and your benefits. Now it is time to get clarity on what tasks you will need to do to make those benefits a reality.

In this step you are going to create a hierarchy diagram to put together all the activities of your project. In project management jargon this is called a work breakdown structure. Creating it will help you understand the complexity of your project and whether or not you will be able to do everything on your own.

Get a pen and paper and do a list of the things you know will need to be done in order to accomplish your project. Do it in the biggest degree of detail first to make sure you account for all the work.

Here you may need to do some online research on

how to do particular things, that is ok. The key is having all the work listed, no matter whether you are an expert on it or not.

To give you an idea here are the tasks I listed to carry out my project.

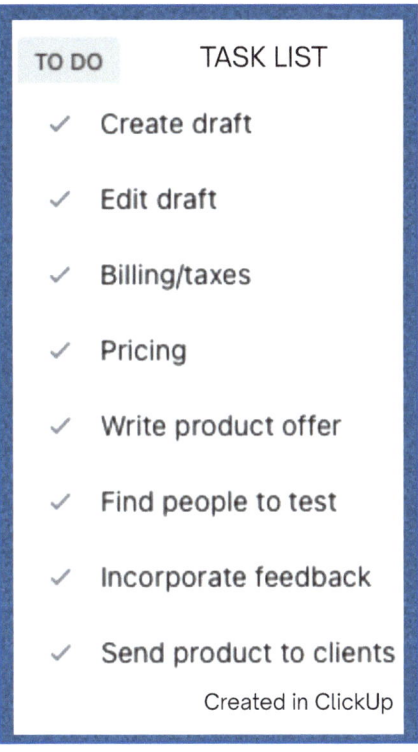

I know some of those tasks can be broken down into smaller pieces. The level of detail you want to get into here is up to you. I didn't go all the way down because I like my hierarchies fairly simple. But also because I do go into a lot more detail when it comes to doing the timelines. However if you are doing a complex project or you are a very visual person I would advise you to get into as

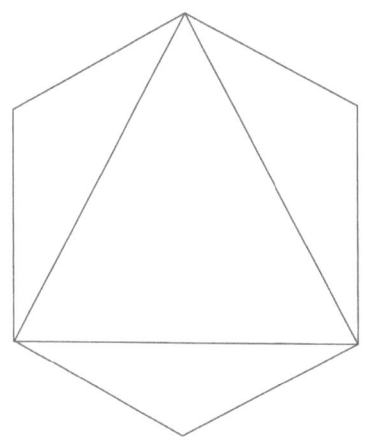

much detail as possible from now. Plus all these details will be super handy when you are doing your timeline, so it won't go to waste.

Now list the activities for your project, with the level of detail you prefer. You can do it on paper for the moment.

When you have done the list go back to your benefits map and check if all the benefits listed there are covered with the tasks you wrote down. This is a good way of ensuring you are not missing any key component of your project.

Now you know all that needs doing, it is time to organise it.

Look at your list and start seeing common themes. These will vary depending on the project you are doing. These themes will be the categories of your project. And then you can bring all together creating a hierarchical diagram:

- the first level is the name of your project

- the second level are the categories you have defined

- the third level are all the relevant tasks of that category

- the fourth level would be subtasks of the tasks on the third level and so on

See an example below based on the work I had to do to create this content you are reading:

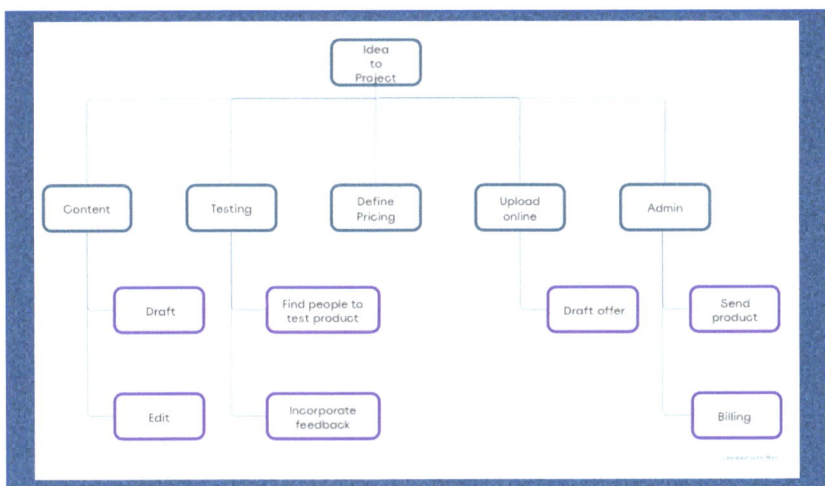

Now is the time for you to do yours. There isn't much point in giving you a template here because the number of branches and boxes is totally up to your project. But you can see the type of structure above and replicate it adapting it to your needs.

Putting all the work in categories allows you to create some structure within your project. You are technically creating the branches of your project tree, on which all the work will be sustained. It will give you clarity.

3.1 SOFTWARE YOU CAN USE

To create the hierarchy above I used the free subscription in Miro. Within that I searched for a template called sitemap. Within that template there are several graphics organised in two columns. I used the second one on the left column. The additional materials document points you to a video so you can find the template too.

Another option you can explore is using ClickUp. In there I would suggest you go into the view mind map to create your hierarchy. You can access the views on the top part of your screen. The only difference is that you will be creating it horizontally rather than vertical. Meaning that the name of your project would be on your left rather than on the top of the diagram.

These are just some options that can save you the time of arranging boxes and lines. However you can do this diagram with any software that allows you to create squares and lines. And just arrange them manually. So Canva (www.canva.com) or any slide creation software can do the trick. And of course pen and paper will work as well too.

4 THE MOTHER OF ALL PROJECT DOCUMENTS

I don't know of any project manager that doesn't have a timeline of some sort for their project. It can be done with more or less level of detail but is a great way of tracking your deadlines and activities, and is the bread and butter of project management.

You are going to build on all the good work you have done so far identifying the tasks for your project.

4.1 SEQUENCING YOUR TASKS

Your next exercise is to make sure you define in which order the tasks have to happen. Sometimes you may have things that you need to do first so another task can commence. For example I can't edit content if I haven't drafted it yet.

But there would be other things that can start on their own accord. Like finding people that want to test my content. I am not saying I need to send it to them at this stage. The task is about finding the volunteers and to do that all I need is an idea of the content that I will create, not the content itself. So I can find my people while I finish off the content. That way I don't have to wait until my content is ready to get people on board. This will both save time and also allow me to keep the momentum going with my project.

I would suggest going over your task list and giving them numbers. Consider whether this task can start on its own or if it needs information from another one. You may have to change the numbers as you go along, don't worry, this is normal and happens to the best project managers.

By the end of this exercise you should have something like this.

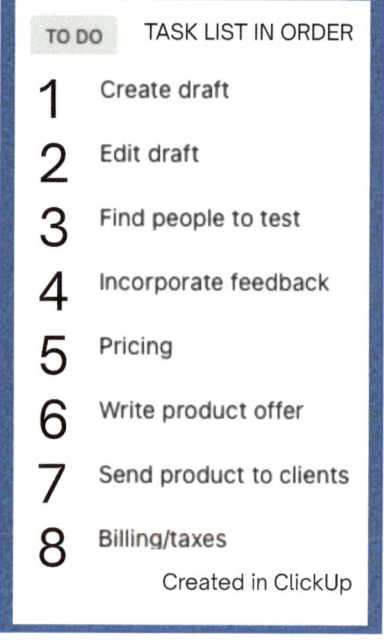

> **Pro tip**
> There is a fine balance between doing things in parallel and creating risks in the project. The more unknowns you have running at the same time the more things you have to be watching out for, which can be time and energy consuming. It can also open the project up to having unexpected changes to try to resolve things without enough certainty. On the other hand doing one activity after another can make a project too long and can delay finding out problems because they get hidden under tasks that you haven't completed yet. Sometimes you don't know what you don't know. To summarise, try to find a reasonable balance when sequencing your tasks.

4.2 TASKS AND TIME SPACE

The next step is understanding how much time each task needs to be completed.

Go over the tasks and assign them a duration. For tasks that you are not sure about you may want to do some online research, talk to friends that may have expertise on that task or just do an estimation.

It is good practice to add a few hours/days to some tasks if you can, in particular those that:

- Are very complex to carry out.

- Are critical to the success of the project, something that if it doesn't get done well will decrease your ability to meet your goal in the way you wanted.

- You are not familiar with, it's always good to have

a buffer when there is uncertainty.

TO DO	TASK LIST IN ORDER WITH DURATIONS	
1	Create draft	2 days
2	Edit draft	4 days
3	Find people to test	3 days
4	Incorporate feedback	3 days
5	Pricing	1 day
6	Write product offer	1 day
7	Send product to clients	1 hour
8	Billing/taxes	1 day a month
	Created in ClickUp with text field for	

4.3 YOUR PROJECT TIMELINE

Now is the time to bring all this together and create the mother of all your project documents. You have all you need already. You just need to make one more decision. What I call your "time strategy".

Do you want to complete your project at that original date no matter what? Or can you have some flexibility with that?

Have a think about that and make a choice.

In your previous exercise you have assigned durations to your tasks, and before that you had put your tasks in order, which means you have an ordered list of tasks and durations. That is the basis of your timeline. It tells you what needs doing and by when.

You most likely have assigned the tasks' duration just thinking about the time that they would take doing on their own.

To make it all work nicely you just have to write down the tasks in the order you gave them but with the dates feeding and adding on each other, depending on whether the task can start on its own or has to wait for some other task to finish before it can start.

In my example my first task started 31st of October (I kid you not!) drafting all this content. I gave it two days to produce the content, meaning the task will finish on 1 November and the following task, editing content will then start on 2 November.

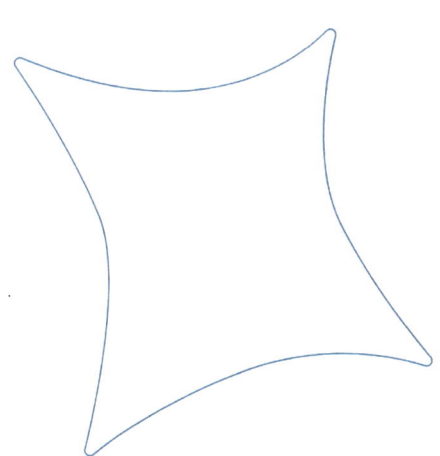

TO DO	TASK LIST WITH DATES	START DATE	DUE DATE
1	Create draft	Today	Tomorrow
2	Edit draft	Tomorrow	Fri
3	Find people to test	Nov 7	Nov 9
4	Incorporate feedback	Nov 9	Nov 11
5	Pricing	Nov 14	Nov 14
6	Write product offer	Nov 15	Nov 15
7	Send product to clients	-	
8	Billing/taxes	-	

Created in ClickUp

Basically you transform the durations into specific dates. And the date your last task ends is the date your project will end.

You made it!

In my example the end date of my project will be 15 November. I have two other tasks associated with the project but those are more of an operational nature. They represent work that I will have to do when the project is live. But they are not required to allow me to put my content online. So I have left them in the list but I don't need to give them deadlines in this exercise.

A very common way of seeing project timelines is in the form of a Gantt chart. Here is an example I created in ClickUp. I introduced all the tasks and gave them start and end dates.

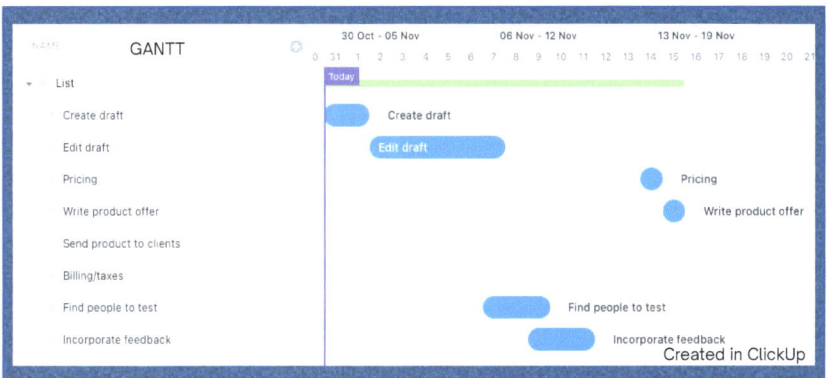
Created in ClickUp

Here is where the question I asked you at the beginning of the chapter comes in. You need to compare the end date of your project with your answer to the second question of the book, several exercises ago. Are they similar? Can you live with any difference? If the answer is yes, move on to the next section.

If you want to make the project shorter, for whatever reason you have two options:

- Review the durations you gave to the tasks to see what savings you can find. Keep in mind doing things quickly can introduce risks and higher costs. In particular if there are activities that you are going to outsource.

- Review the sequencing of tasks to see if you can start tasks sooner. For example I could wait to have all my drafts done before I start editing. But I could also start editing what I have and do the editing in parallel with the drafting as tasks. This may take less time overall, but it would also introduce the risks that some of the editing I do goes to waste if I decide to change the content before finishing the whole drafting. There is always a give and take when adjusting timelines

4.4 MONEY TIME

Now you have your timeline, the last bit you need to understand all the basics of your project is how much it would cost to carry it out.

We often do this after having a timeline because you need to know how long things take to be able to price them up.

Consider the following aspects when doing this:

- How valuable is your own time? Don't assume because you will be doing a task of your project it won't cost you anything. If you are the one carrying it out you won't be able to do other activities that may actually bring you far more benefits either personally or professionally.

- Do you want to meet that final date at all costs? That will probably require you a higher budget so you can throw money at tasks and problems to get them fixed quicker.

Go over your timeline and start calculating the cost of each task. Give yourself a daily/hourly fee for the duration of the tasks. Use the fee of a team member or a freelancer if you have it. For some tasks you may want to request quotes to be as precise as possible. Others may be part of subscriptions or services you use for several projects. In that case you can spread that cost proportionally so each project contributes towards that expense.

TO DO		BUDGET
1	Create draft	£100
2	Edit draft	£150
3	Find people to test	£50
4	Incorporate feedback	£200
5	Pricing	£50
6	Write product offer	£50
7	Send product to clients	£3
8	Billing/taxes	£50

Created in ClickUp

Also you need to consider that sometimes a task may take a certain period of time but that doesn't mean you have to be on the task all the time. For example, my task of finding people to test this content is going to take 4 days. Out of those four days there will be times when I will be on the task, sending messages. Most of the task time is going to be taken up by the time people take to get back to me, which is a delay but doesn't necessarily mean I am dedicated fully to the task. As you define more projects you get used to these nuances and how to include them in the documentation.

Once you have your costs you can do an estimate of the income this project would generate and subtract the costs from it. This may help you get an idea of the economic gain, which sometimes can be a deciding factor. If you have several ideas waiting to be brought to life you could use this exercise to prioritise them. However, if possible you should also consider other factors such as how much you are going to enjoy carrying out the project, which project is going to give you more satisfaction once it is completed, etc. as deciding factors.

> **Pro tip**
> If you are able I would strongly recommend adding a contingency budget to the overall budget. The amount of money you put in this pot could be anything between 5% for projects that you are very familiar with and have little risk and 40% for projects with high amounts of uncertainty and risk.

You are all sorted, you have your key documents for a project, in a simple way.

You have transformed your idea into a project!

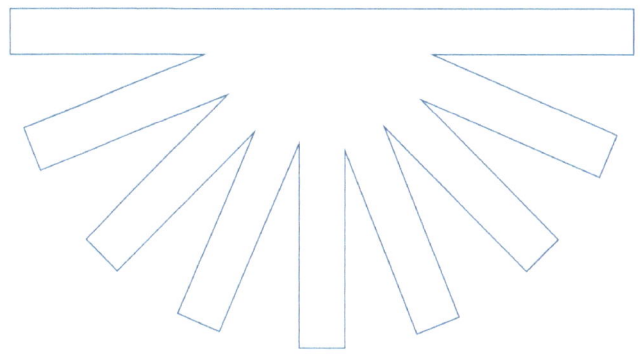

4.5 SOFTWARE YOU CAN USE

I can't think about timelines or Gantt charts without very famous commercial products coming to mind. This is probably because when I started in project management there weren't as many options as there are now. Plus those two tend to be used in big companies and the public sector. These systems allow you to create the tasks, assign durations and costs so it all gets built in together. However they are not free to use and for the purpose of what you are doing here you may not need them.

Over recent years a lot of new project management tools focused on online projects have come to life. Asana is a fairly easy one to use and their free plan is useful.

You can also use ClickUp. Create a space with the name of your project. Then you can add tasks and subtasks. You can also give them durations. Once you have all that set up you can go to the Gantt view and see the tasks in the form of a timeline. In the additional material document you will find a video on how to do it.

Miro also has an option to build a Gantt chart visually. It is one of the templates they provide. I find it a bit tedious to use but it is a free option that is there. And if you want to have all your project documents only in one site that may be a good choice. You can do decent benefits maps and hierarchies there too.

5 WHAT COMES NEXT

You've made it. Your idea is not an idea anymore. It is now a project. You know what you are going to achieve, how and by when. How exciting!

Now is the time to crack on with doing it. The managing of the project if you will. That is another aspect of project management and it revolves a lot about leadership, communication and problem solving.

In my experience project definition tends to be quite unique to the project at hand. You apply the same principles to get the structure no matter the type of project but you often encounter different challenges or new things when you are defining your project.

Managing a project tends to be similar no matter the project subject, because at the end of the day you are always managing a team of people doing tasks.

Whilst the managing of the project is outside of the scope of what I am doing here I will give you a few tips:

- Always do your best to manage people the way you would like to be managed.

- If you have several people involved in your project define and agree who is going to be doing what as soon as possible. You can search online for RACI, a roles and responsibility type of document that will help you avoid miscommunications and ensure that all tasks will be done.

- Understand that your team is made of humans and being a leader means knowing how to connect with your team. The best way I found of getting someone to be productive and motivated is ensuring they feel valued and have what they need to do their job. Sometimes that is a physical resource, and sometimes that is an open and honest conversation or an activity outside of work to see each other as humans.

- Be flexible in your leadership style. Don't use a blanket approach on how you manage people. Flow between directing, monitoring, coaching and mentoring depending on the amount of experience of your team member on that task in particular. The way you are going to manage them should be agreed with them from the start so everyone is clear about the team dynamics.

- Be open, honest, clear and concise in communications. Always seek clarification when in doubt. Seeking opinions from stakeholders is a great way of building support, identifying risks or gaps and getting everyone on the same page.

- Manage information wisely. Identify who needs to know what and when. Sometimes telling something to a key stakeholder in the right moment can make all the difference.

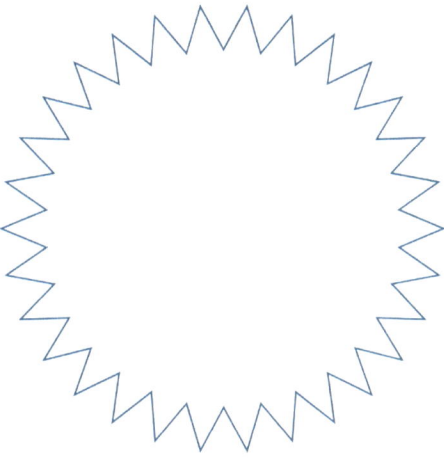

- Celebrate successes as you go through the project. It is great to keep up momentum and stay motivated. Don't celebrate only at the end!

6 YOUR MINDSET

The previous chapters have outlined a series of steps you can follow to transform an idea into an action plan. The difference between having a plan and actually following through with it it's, more often than not, your mindset.

Do you believe you are capable of doing this work? Do you believe that things work in your favour? Because no matter how well organised you are, if you don't believe you can do it the road will be much more difficult. Not impossible but for sure it would be harder than it could be. You will need to put more effort and energy into each step. That often leads to frustration and disappointment, which can end in abandoning an idea, even before the project to create it has been completed or even started.

This is why I am adding this chapter. To help you work with your mind so that your inner voice gets on board with your idea as much as possible.

Think about your mind in this extremely simplistic way, as if it only had two parts. A part focused on daily life and another one underneath it.

The day to day part is often in the driver seat, helping you analysing situations, making decisions, going about your life, etc.

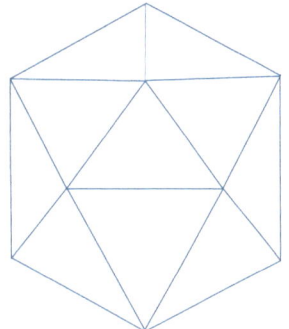

And the part that lives underneath is the one sometimes whispering you doubts or fears. Things like: don't bother, it's too much effort, you are not good enough to make this work, life is too hard...This part is a mix of all the past experiences you had in your life, the culture you absorbed from your environment, even beliefs from your family that got passed on to you. All these create a series of black boxes, full of memories, feelings and decisions you made at those times to try to make sense of what was happening and how you were feeling.

Not all the decisions you made in the past had to be logical. The objective of this part of your mind is avoiding feeling discomfort again, at all costs. Logic is not necessarily part of that equation. Your mind will create decisions and beliefs to fulfil this purpose. This can translate into creating situations where you reaffirm those beliefs, because the pain known is better than the unknown. Or preventing you from being in a situation like that again. Because inaction altogether is a much safer bet than doing something and not going your way.

For example, perhaps when you were a child you had a great idea about drawing. You did it and showed it to your caretakers or teachers. But they didn't react the way you wanted. They didn't tell you how good the drawing was or how talented you were or how proud they were that you did this. One of the many ways your mind can interpret that is creating the belief that you are not creative, that your drawing isn't good, that is why they didn't appreciate what you did. And therefore there is no point in following up with any creative idea anymore because that is just not you. You are not gonna get recognised by it, so why risk doing something, putting all that much effort to get disappointed again.

That could be one of the many scenarios that could be interfering with your ability to create something, to start or complete a project. The number of scenarios here is quite high. There are many types of memories, feelings and beliefs that can be blocking you.

With the power of will and a lot of energy you can push through and get stuff done.
But there is a simple way to start uncovering and releasing all these boxes so they don't affect you so much. That will be a much easier way of going

about things than having to power through all the time.

Plus if you do this, not only you will improve your chances of completing your project. You will also be healing parts of yourself through the process.

I love projects, I think they are the vehicles for change and growth. And I strongly believe as much as they can deliver business growth and abundance of all sorts, they can also be spaces for personal growth.

This chapter aims exactly at that. Achieving healing and personal growth through your idea.
This approach means you are not only delivering good into the world, you are also delivering more good to yourself. Two for the price of one.

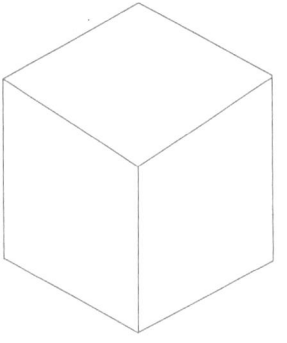

To do this, grab pen and paper and do the below exercises, answering the questions in that order. Before each question take a deep breath, one that goes directly into your belly and expands it. Journal whatever answer you get. Don't judge it. If a question doesn't bring anything up that is absolutely fine.

The questions are grouped by themes. Some days

one theme may be more fruitful than another one. That's ok and perfectly normal. The key is doing this work so you become aware of whatever thought, feeling or limiting belief is showing up in your life at this point in time. Once you gain awareness you will feel more empowered and you will be able to consciously work on releasing it.

> **EXERCISE 1**
> Think about your idea, do you feel any resistance about it happening how you want?
> 1. What does that mean about you? About life?
> 2. When did you feel like this before?
> 3. What happened?
> 4. What decision did you make about you? About life? About your ability to create things?

> **EXERCISE 2**
> Imagine your idea has become a reality how you wanted
> 1. How are you feeling?
> 2. What does that mean about you?
> 3. When did you feel like this before?
> 4. What happened?
> 5. What decision did you make about you? About life? About your ability to create things?

> **EXERCISE 3**
> Now imagine your idea has happened but not the way you wanted
> 1. How are you feeling?
> 2. What does that mean about you?
> 3. What does that mean about life, the world?
> 4. What does that mean about your ability to create?
> 5. When did you feel like this before?
> 6. What happened?
> 7. What would have liked to happen instead?

EXERCISE 4
Think about the last time you tried to create something and it didn't happen how you wanted
1. How are you feeling about it right now?
2. How did you feel about it then?
3. What does that mean about you?
4. What decision did you make about your ability to create?
5. What do you need to hear, see, experience to let that go?
6. How can you give yourself that so you can move on?

EXERCISE 5
Think about a time you created something and you didn't receive the support you wanted
1. What happened?
2. Who didn't support you (parent, family, friends, customers)?
3. How do you feel about that?
4. What does that mean about you as a creator?
5. What does that mean about them?
6. What does that mean about life, the universe?
7. What decision did you make about following up on your ideas?

EXERCISE 6
Think about a time you created something and it went exactly as you wanted
1. What happened?
2. How did you feel?
3. What did that mean about you then?
4. What decisions did you make as a result of that experience?
5. How you feel now looking back?
6. What does that past event mean about you now?

To help you let go of all this unnecessary stuff you can play the meditation from the additional material document. It will help you connect with your idea at a deeper level and work on the interference that is showing up.

This work is a first contact with the area of personal growth. Here are a few things to consider, if you are not familiar with this type of work.

6.1 YOUR MIND IS NOT YOUR ENEMY

That part of your mind that makes all those decisions is just trying to protect you from feeling pain. Many people say we should ignore our ego, subjugate it and just power through. I believe our ego is a part of us and we should embrace it. Find a way to work together.

You can do that by giving it a space to voice its feelings. That doesn't necessarily mean you go about screaming at people that hurt you. You can journal about it, say those things out loud when you are alone, etc. Once that part of you has expressed itself it would be much easier to bring them along in your journey. To find a compromise.

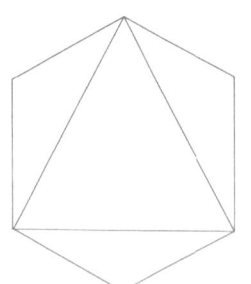

Communicate with that part of yourself often, let them see you are there for them. Because two integrated parts accomplish more than one.

You are working to bring an idea to life. I don't know anyone in a project management position that hasn't had times of feeling not good enough. You do your best to keep things in control, to plan, to foresee what can go wrong. However, one day a teammate misses a deadline. It can be because there was an unforeseen situation or an emergency came up. As a project manager your mind can quickly go into "I should have thought of this before", "I should have made a plan".

From there it can quickly escalate into "I am not good at my job". The other type of response can be you feeling resentment and anger towards that teammate. Regardless of which scenario you are in, here it's when it can be extremely important to explore and voice those feelings in a conscious and healthy way. Journal about your feelings about your ability to manage the project. Then explore if you have any feelings about the person that didn't deliver or any other aspect of the situation that brought you to this point. Release as much of that, deep dive into where it can all be coming from. When did you feel like this before? And then find a way to release it.

It can be that you make a list of all the good things you have done during your management of this project, all the saves you caught. This can help you remind yourself you are good enough, it is just that there isn't anyone perfect.

You can also write a letter explaining your frustration at your teammate or the situation. You don't need to send it. It is just a tool to let those emotions flow out of your system.

Or maybe you find another way of releasing this that works for you. The important thing is integrating the two aspects of your mind so they can work together.

6.2 THE PROCESS DELIVERS RESULTS IN THE LONG RUN

Opening those boxes and experiencing feelings may be weird and may feel pointless at first. However once you get used to it you will see how much better you feel without all that stuffed inside. It is a great tool for personal wellness.

Looking into your personal growth will bring you confidence and more inner peace when managing projects. At least it did to me. You will be more resilient in scenarios when things don't go according to plan. When remaining calm and confident is a 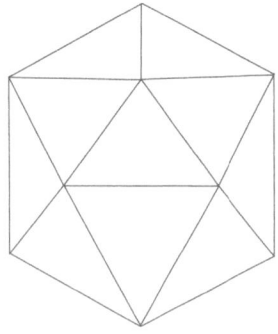 huge asset. You will approach situations that would have been stressful in the past with more calm and groundedness. Which will make you more resourceful.

As you become more self-aware you will also be able to have more compassion towards yourself and others. You will be able to broaden your perspective and take things less personally. This can be a great source of peace on its own.

6.3 INNER WORK IS ABOUT TAKING RESPONSIBILITY

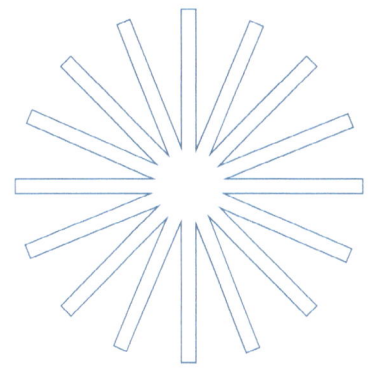

Self-awareness implies being accountable for your emotions, beliefs and feelings.

This doesn't have anything to do with feeling guilt, blame or shame about anything that you have experienced. It is about the fact that no matter what has happened to you, you are the only person capable of addressing how you feel about it. You don't release painful memories or forgive to benefit others, you are doing it to benefit yourself. So you don't have to hold on to that stuff anymore.

In every interaction there is 50% of your energy being exchanged. Sometimes we trigger others without meaning to. The same can happen to you. If you are having a conscious polite conversation about a trigger and someone tells you I felt in this particular way be kind enough to look within and check whether anything related to that could be living inside of you.

For example I used to trigger a teammate a lot. For him the way I talked when managing the project was very demanding and controlling, even when I said things with a please and in a normal tone of voice. It would have been very easy for me to say that it's his problem and he has to sort himself out. We are our own responsibility after all.

But I went within and I explored whether a part of me needed to control things for any particular reason since he was having that experience when interacting with me. And when I did it I realised I still had stuff to release about not feeling safe (hence the need for control). That need for control was being projected through my words without me realising and it was triggering for someone that had to heal stuff about feeling controlled.

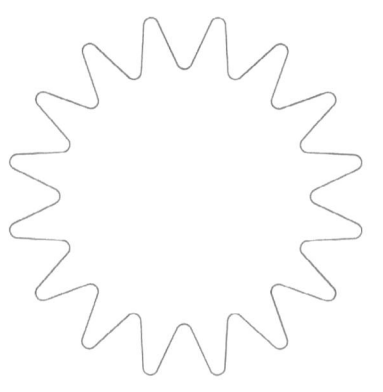

That is how the 50-50 works. There is healing on both sides, we just have to be brave enough to always look within.

And of course if you go within and you don't find anything to heal on your side, perhaps there isn't anymore. Then it would be a case of just being ok with the other person saying whatever they are saying. Perhaps their journey requires that. If you have gone in and checked at least you know you have done as much as possible.

6.4 THERE IS ALWAYS A LESSON, A GIFT

When you are working on releasing a limiting belief you basically uncover a lesson for yourself.

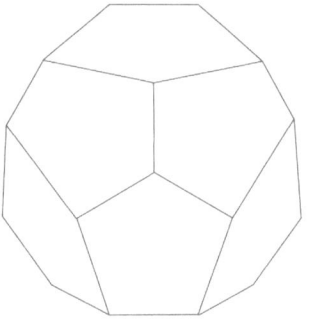

For example, in the situation I referred to earlier about my need for control, the lesson for me is that now I was actually safe and I didn't have to control everything around me. That I could trust myself and life to have my back. This brings feelings of trust and safety into my awareness, which are the opposite theme to what I was keeping inside. And means now I can feel safe and it feels very brightly and strongly.

In turn that allowed me to empower my team more and give them more space to do their work. Which translated into them feeling more valued. And that is a great environment for collaboration and productivity in any project.

Often the lesson with inner work is about duality. How we have experienced one side of the coin and when we let that side go we get to the other side, which tends to be a nice experience. And because we know what it is to feel the lack of, feeling the positive side feels much sweeter and empowering. The lessons also offer us opportunities for our team and projects, like in my case creating a more empowering work environment.

6.5 TRIGGERS ARE GROWTH OPPORTUNITIES

Getting upset or triggered shouldn't be only about blaming others: you said this and now I feel x.

During one of my projects a teammate was constantly finding fault at my work and my English skills. Though English is not my mother tongue, I had never in my previous 6 years of professional experience in the United Kingdom been told my English wasn't good enough or my work was lacking. As you can imagine his comments made me feel not good enough in a very big way.

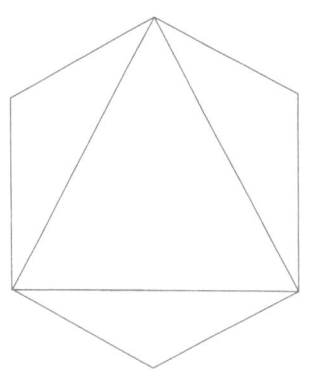 I checked with my colleagues and manager to see if I was missing the mark with my current performance level. They all said it was not on me, it was him that was off point. So I went in and explored how I was feeling and what all this meant to me. I discovered these triggers were feeling so strongly because they were pointing me towards my own limiting belief that I wasn't good enough.

Every time he was saying anything of that sort to me he was reaffirming that personal belief that I had about myself. And because I didn't want to feel that way about myself I was getting angry at him.

Granted he was not acting in a very polite way but part of the problem was what I was actually believing inside of me. Once I discovered what was hiding underneath all of this I worked on my own limiting belief. Releasing those fears that I was not good enough. Remembering all the good stuff I had accomplished in life. I found a deeper sense of inner confidence and fulfilment. More importantly I was able to not care regardless of what my teammate said to me anymore. The trigger was made void. This is the beauty of personal growth.

After I did all that inner work it was also much easier to express myself and set boundaries with this teammate. I could speak about it without my words being charged because I had sorted my side of things beforehand. It is much better to set limits once the emotional situation has been at least partly defused.

When you get triggered you have a golden opportunity to figure out what is underneath all that and heal that part of yourself. If you do, the next time you are in a similar situation it won't hurt as much and that is an incredible gift.

Of course this doesn't excuse bad behaviour, we shouldn't be telling people horrible things just because we feel them. The funny thing is sometimes we get triggered regardless of whether there were bad words exchanged or the intention of those words. That is because there is some limiting belief or painful memory acting inside of you. If you are meant to heal, you will be set off even with a hug or a kind word. I know it because it has happened to me too!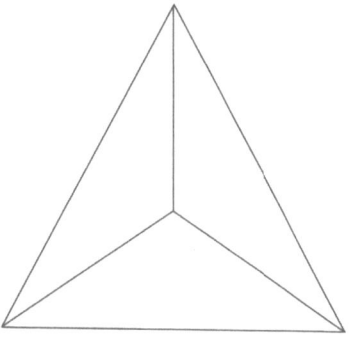

At the same time this doesn't condone receiving any abuse. If you keep being at the end of abusive behaviour things have to change and boundaries have to be set. You can work on yourself as much as you can as I mentioned in my example above. But sometimes part of the healing is taking action, realising you are good enough and deserve to be treated with love and respect and set limits accordingly. No amount of healing or inner work excuses abusive behaviour.

6.6 YOUR ARE WORKING WITH INVISIBLE THINGS

Doing inner work means working with emotions, thoughts and feelings. Those are aspects of ourselves that live in the invisible world since they are not necessarily 3D objects that we can see easily with our human eyes. A very important aspect of fully releasing a limiting belief is taking an action in the "real world" that would diminish the influence of that limiting belief, contrasting its power sort of speak.

For example, if I am working on a limiting belief that I am not good enough to write a book and publish it, one of the best ways I have to disprove that belief is actually writing a book and publishing it. Your project will surely offer 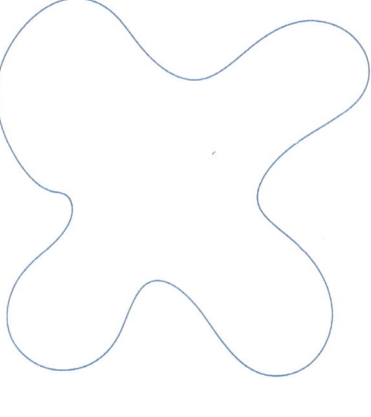 you opportunities to challenge your own perceptions about yourself through the completion of some tasks or managing certain team members successfully. That can be a great tool for personal growth.

Always try to find a way to do the opposite to what your mind is saying to prove that part of yourself that actually you are more than what your mind says. It is a great way of releasing limiting beliefs. Just exercise some sensible caution, don't go jumping off rooftops trying to prove you can fly on your own! In that case your mind may be right!

6.7 FINDING KINDNESS

Be kind towards yourself and others. As a project manager you are in a unique position not only to find personal growth as you manage the project but to facilitate the same for your team. You are a human being with things going on in your life and work is just part of that mix. The same is for your teammates.

We all have stuff to go through. All we can do is be willing to do that work and create a space for others to do the same. In my experience your team will respect you even more when you can support them in their journey and you see them as humans. They notice you are on their side and it will make it natural for them to be productive and support the project.

Of course you may need to be assertive from time

 to time to ensure roles and responsibilities are clear. And all this doesn't imply you are not going to look after your timeline and the deadlines. But for me project management shouldn't be just about chasing people up for stuff. Projects are a great opportunity to achieve business goals and also create personal growth for all involved. That will transform work environments into something more, a place you really want to be in everyday because you get more out of it than just improving your cv. And who doesn't want to manage and work on projects like that.

If you have questions managing your project you can always reach out and have a coaching or consulting session.

All the best of luck in this project and in any other endeavour.

ABOUT THE AUTHOR

My name is Ines Lopez. I have over 10 years of experience in project management. I lead projects of up to £300m in many types of areas: transportation, urban realm, environment, renewable energy, startups and culture. I also have a Masters of Science in Strategic Project Management if credentials are your thing.

The bit I like the most is the early days, when all you have is a goal and you need to sort out how you are going to make it happen. Over the last five years I have specialised myself in that part of the project cycle and personal development. I have helped many people bring their ideas to life in a simple way. And I would like to inspire even more projects into reality.

The world needs you to create that idea that has been living in your brain. Otherwise you wouldn't have it in the first place.

If you want to discuss coaching or consulting for your project use the QR code or visit **https://linktr.ee/elements.artist** to see all the ways to find me.

www.ingramcontent.com/pod-product-compliance
Lightning Source LLC
Chambersburg PA
CBHW040327220526
45473CB00009B/2593